JUST LIGHTEN UP!

A Coloring Book for Children and Adults

Written & Illustrated
by Leia Stinnett

Other Books by Leia Stinnett:

A Circle of Angels
All My Angel Friends
The Twelve Universal Laws

The Little Angel Books Series:

Animal Tales: Spiritual Lessons from Our Animal Friends
The Angel Told Me to Tell You Good-bye
The Bridge Between Two Worlds
Color Me One
Crystals R for Kids
Exploring the Chakras
Happy Feet
One Red Rose
When the Earth Was New
Where Is God?
Who's Afraid of the Dark?

Cover art
by Leia Stinnett

ISBN 0-929385-64-0
Published by
StarChild Press
a division of
Light Technology Publishing
P.O. Box 1526, Sedona, AZ 86339

Printed by
MISSION POSSIBLE
Commercial Printing
P.O. Box 1495
Sedona, AZ 86339

DEDICATION

Just Lighten Up! is dedicated to everyone in the world who has ever had a bad day. On one such occasion I met Mobley, one of the "Lighten Up" Angels, who reminded me that life is an opportunity for us to experience joy, laughter, love, peace and harmony.

Each little angel in this coloring book is demonstrating a tool we can all use to help us lighten up during the day. If we really want to be grumpy and unhappy, we can. But it is very difficult to stay that way when the Lighten Up Angels start revealing themselves in our lives.

So call on these angels. Ask them to laugh and play with you, to help you see the humor in all experiences you create. Release negative thoughts, feelings and emotions as you color these lighthearted little angel pictures. Laughter *is* the best "medicine," and these little angels can brighten any day!

"Just Lighten Up"

These little angels
are coming your way
With one special mission –
let's brighten the day.

So often we judge
what we see as imperfect
We are mad at the world
We have no respect.

But sadness and anger
make our day go all wrong
We can change what we think
through dance and a song.

To see that we're happy
God brings us a gift
so we can find love
Our moods then can shift.

Lighten up, lighten up!
There's no reason to pout
No reason to cry,
No reason to doubt!

Let these Lighten Up Angels
    move into your heart
So each new day you experience
    brings a fresh start!

They tell you keep smiling
    and never be down,
Put a smile on your face, now
    away goes that frown.

Eat chocolate hearts.

Give yourself a big hug.

See the light.

Talk to God.

Create . . .

Take time to smell the flowers.

Talk to a friend.

Blow bubbles.

Swing on a star.

Have an adventure.

Read a good book.

Play in the rain.

Go surfing.

Build castles in the sand.

Learn to juggle.

Go for a ride.

Throw away all your cares.

Dare to dream.

Go shopping.

Go on vacation.

Learn ballet.

Sing with the angels.

Catch a falling star.

Talk to a tree.

Go fishing.

Play your favorite game.

Spend time with a pet.

Take a bubble bath.

Check out some clouds.

Try windsailing.

Dress in something wild and crazy.

Go for a swim.

Have a party.

Take a short nap.

Try a new look.

Look at things in a different way.

Laugh at yourself.

Think positive thoughts.

Celebrate you!

Take things in stride.

Just be.

About the Author

The '80s were a decade of self-discovery for Leia Stinnett after she began researching many different avenues of spirituality. In her profession as a graphic designer she had become restless, knowing there was something important she had to do outside the materiality of corporate America.

In August 1986 Leia had her first contact with Archangel Michael when he appeared in a physical form of glowing blue light. A voice said, "I am Michael. Together we will save the children."

In 1988 she was inspired by Michael to teach spiritual classes in Sacramento, California, the Circle of Angels. Through these classes she had the opportunity to work with learning-disabled children, children of abuse and those from dysfunctional homes.

Later Michael told her, "Together we are going to write the Little Angel Books." To date Leia and Michael have created fifteen Little Angel Books that present various topics of spiritual truths and principles. The books proved popular among adults as well as children.

The Circle of Angels classes have been introduced to several countries around the world and across the U.S., and Leia and her husband Douglas now have a teacher's manual and training program for people who wish to offer spiritual classes to children. Leia and Michael have been interviewed on Canadian Satellite TV and have appeared on NBC-TV's *Angels II – Beyond the Light,* which featured their Circle of Angels class and discussed their books and Michael's visit.

The angels have given Leia and Douglas a vision of a new educational system without competition or grades — one that supports love and positive self-esteem, honoring all children as the independent lights they are. Thus they are now writing a curriculum for the new "schools of light" and developing additional books and programs for children.